AIDAN'S
AWESOME
ADVENTURES

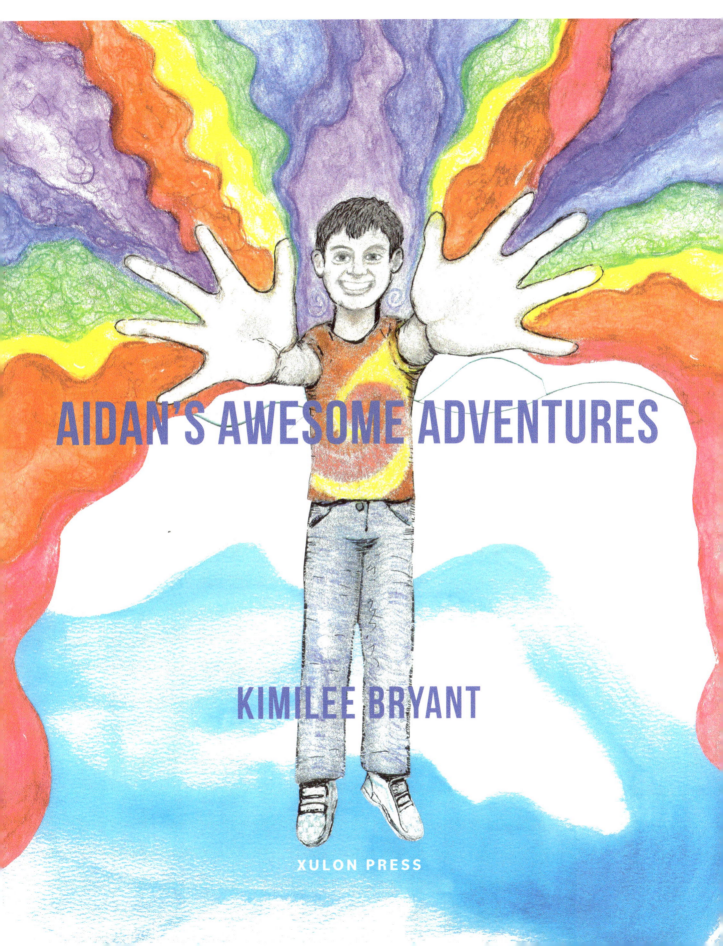

Xulon Press
555 Winderley Pl, Suite 225
Maitland, FL 32751
407.339.4217
www.xulonpress.com

© 2024 by Kimilee Bryant
Illustrations by Andrew Bryant

All rights reserved solely by the author. The author guarantees all contents are original and do not infringe upon the legal rights of any other person or work. No part of this book may be reproduced in any form without the permission of the author.

Due to the changing nature of the Internet, if there are any web addresses, links, or URLs included in this manuscript, these may have been altered and may no longer be accessible. The views and opinions shared in this book belong solely to the author and do not necessarily reflect those of the publisher. The publisher therefore disclaims responsibility for the views or opinions expressed within the work.

Paperback ISBN-13: 979-8-86850-365-8
Ebook ISBN-13: 979-8-86850-366-5

Dedicated to "Gypsy" and Aunt Corinne Hovda and in honor of Karen Cromer "Gran" Bryant

I am Kimilee, Aidan's mom. I teach singing, acting, piano, and dance lessons. My students call me "Miss Kimilee"

Aidan doesn't talk much, except when we ask him questions, so let's ask:

What is your name?

"My name is Aidan."

How old are you?

"I'm nine years old."

Where do you live?

"Greenville, South Carolina."

What is your mommy's name?

"Kimilee Bryant."

What is your favorite color?

"My favorite color is... blue!"

Do you have a dog?

"Yes."

What is her name?

"Gypsy."

Aidan loves roller coasters, swimming, and dancing.

He has been to many theme parks, but mostly to Disney World in Florida where he likes to see many fairy tale characters like Cinderella, Peter Pan, and The Little Mermaid.

His favorite princess is Tiana from *The Princess and the Frog.*

Aidan has a condition called Autism Spectrum Disorder, or "ASD." We learned that he had this when he was about two years old. He will always have this; it doesn't go away. Aidan learns and communicates differently from his friends at school, but he learns and knows just as much and tries really hard!

Picture by Aidan and Uncle Andrew

His friends at school are really kind and help him when they can. They hold his hand and help keep him calm when he feels overwhelmed by noise or too much information.

He really loves them, especially Shay, Charlotte, Hannah, Addison, and Bryson. His buddy, Caden, says he's his "bodyguard."

Another friend, Chase, helped him with his microphone when Aidan had a solo in chorus.

Yes, Aidan got a solo! I was so excited since I am a singer myself! Since Aidan doesn't really talk much and doesn't like to sing *with* everyone (even though he loves being *in* chorus), I did not expect him to get the solo! All of his friends told his teacher, Mrs. C, that Aidan should get the solo. About fifty kids auditioned, but Mrs. C said Aidan would do it at the spring school concert! The song was about being brave, strong, loved, smart, and unique. Aidan is definitely all of those things! I bet you are, too!

Do you have friends who learn differently? Do they sometimes have unique behaviors?

Aidan sometimes hums at a very high pitch and likes to hold onto objects like a plastic hanger or an old bubble wand. This is called "stimming," which means that he repeats movements of his body or sounds that he makes. It helps him feel better and deal with stressful situations. We all do it, but it might look different. Twirling hair, biting nails, or even just watching TV can be a "stim." Some people with autism flap their hands or repeat words over and over (this is also called "scripting").

Have you ever said the words of a song or recited a book or poem to yourself? Maybe you have practiced "scripting," too!

There are now (in 2024) 1 in 36 children diagnosed on the autism spectrum, so chances are you know someone that is like Aidan.

*Statistic taken from the 2024 CDC website.

Just like all of your friends, though, we are ALL different; even people diagnosed with ASD are all different. Dr. Stephen Shore once said, "If you've met one person with autism, you've met one person with autism." Some folks talk, and some don't.

Aidan's "stims" might be different from his friends, just like how you might like ballet and your friend likes basketball.

Some people on the spectrum don't like to go places, but right now, Aidan loves to go on adventures! New York City, where he was born, is one of his favorite places where he likes to visit museums, parks, and Broadway.

Mommy is an opera singer and worked on Broadway in a big show, which is why Aidan was born in New York City.

Now, we live in South Carolina near our family and we travel a lot to the beach and to Florida.

Aidan always tells us the capital of each state wherever we travel. Albany is the capital of New York, Harrisburg is the capital of Pennsylvania, Columbia is the capital of South Carolina, Atlanta is the capital of Georgia, and Tallahassee is the capital of Florida.

He has been to other states, but has mostly only seen them from within the car, so we have many more adventures waiting for us! California and Hawaii are next on our list!

A very famous autistic person, Dr. Temple Grandin, said, "I'm different, not less." Next time you see or hear someone who is different, be kind and consider learning how you can help them and how they might even help you. It might be a great adventure!